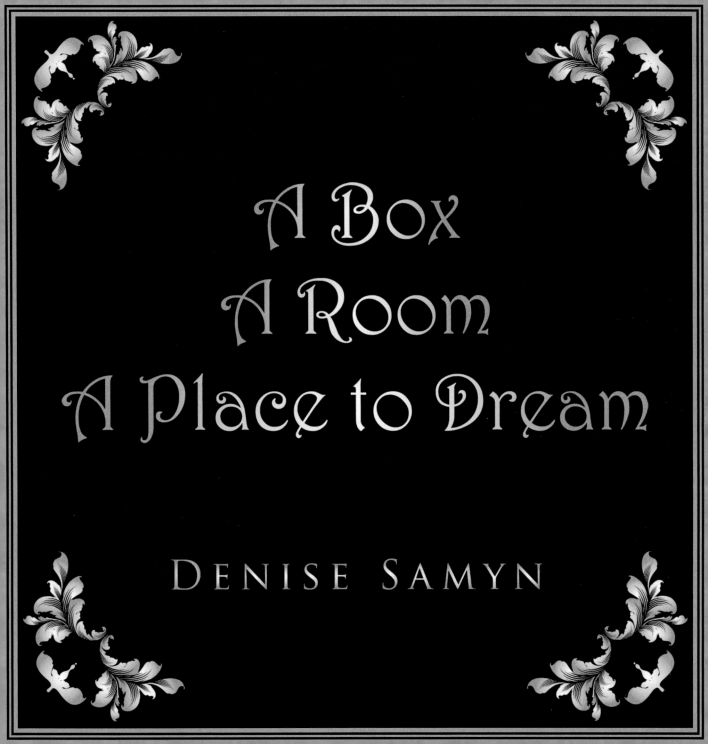

A Box
A Room
A Place to Dream

DENISE SAMYN

Order this book online at www.trafford.com
or email orders@trafford.com

Most Trafford titles are also available at major online book retailers.

Printed in the United States of America.

ISBN: 978-1-4907-2270-2 (sc)
978-1-4907-2271-9 (e)

Library of Congress Control Number: 2013923803

Trafford rev. 12/30/2013

Trafford
PUBLISHING® www.trafford.com

North America & international
toll-free: 1 888 232 4444 (USA & Canada)
fax: 812 355 4082

This book could not have happened without the love and support from my parents, Robert and Rebecca Bell, whom I miss so much and think about each and every day. Also to my loving husband, Filiep, who has supported me throughout the entire process. His love and guidance has been a blessing. To my siblings: Larry, Wanda, Robert, Teresa, Maria, Timothy, Angela, Tracy, and Terry, whom I love and miss, but mostly to the Creator of all light and life. The belief in a power greater than myself has given me the strength needed to complete this book.

Thank you.

Introduction

When you open a book, you open up a world of possibilities, of ideas and viewpoints.

This is the introduction to a compilation of poems—these are a lifetime of expressions, ideas, and observations by me entitled *A Box, A Room, A Place to Dream*.

The book consists of free-form and multi-formed poems and is a dream come true. In the beginning, it was a way for me to express myself, and I find great comfort in writing.

Now, I realize it's time to share my work with the rest of the world.

If you have a dream, then make it happen. Believe in yourself and in your abilities and to bring your dreams to fruition. Never allow fear to hinder you.

A Place to Dream

Look around you

See what is there

Be inquisitive and dare

Visualize your dreams

Then make them come true

This world is yours

The time is now for you

Golden Garden

Like the yellow softness of a daffodil or the smell of a fresh new morn,
you uplift my heart and my soul.

Like the rays of light that fall from the sun to brighten the leaves and stems, you warm me.

No longer shall I fear the darkness that envelops me from time to time
or the deafening sounds of life that permeate the winds,

For I have found the golden garden in your eyes, your voice, your touch.

A Winged, Wicked Tongue

Lies spill from twisted lips

Paranoia stains the mind

Hatred and dangerous idioms hemorrhage from

A winged, wicked tongue

Fragmented lives, detached hearts, suspicion, spite,
and superstition all spawned from

A winged wicked tongue.

Loves forever lost, harmony dissolved, and phobias breed.

Uneasiness surrounds and unpleasantness abounds

From place to place.

From face to face travels

A winged wicked tongue

Africa's Seed

From moon to moon, bright sky to night

From grand-mother to grand-daughter, great-grandfather to grand-son

Africa's seed survives

Through famine, disease, bondage, and tribal wars

Through drought, oppression, and assassination

Africa's seed survives

And though the seed grows weak and is undernourished

Ambition with education, pride with a purpose, and determination without end

Africa's seed will continue to survive

Africa Weeps

The motherland is weeping.

Can you hear her tears?

While famine consumes her young

And disease cripples her population,

Africa weeps.

Pollution destroys the precious life-giving waters.

Poachers kill the endangered.

Others strip the land of the precious gems held so dear by those of foreign lands.

Politicians bargain and debate; still civil strife remains.

Hatred of clans is not unfamiliar here, and

Africa weeps.

Help her. Save her.

Remove the shroud of tears from her massive face and birth her return.

AmeriCry

In the land of milk and honey, things are not going well.

Babies are dying.

Violence is tolerated.

Distraught youth and elderly are without hope.

The sandwich generation desperately tries to cope.

Education is starving, priorities abstracted.

In this place, confusion is the norm.

Many are distracted by the lies fed to them by people who cannot tell the truth.

Are we prisoners in a racist and corrupt land who can only dream of nirvana?

As Cisco Sleeps

Tossing and turning with nostrils flared in dreams as he lays in noisy slumber.

Angry lips with eyes closed tight to shut out realities bite as he lies in boisterous slumber.

Like the dolphin that swims on the waves, he moves shifting, squirming, thrashing his body while he lies in uncontrollable slumber.

Be There

I would love to be there when you open your eyes at first light.

I want to be there when you have that 1st cup of coffee of the day.

I need to be there when pain has filled your heart so that I can chase it away.

I want to be there to see you achieve your dreams.

I would love to be there to give advice or to help you see with a different pair of eyes.

But my time has ended here. I may not be here in body, but I will always be with you in spirit.

Be

Be somebody's first time.

Be somebody's one and only.

Be somebody's dream.

Be somebody's hero.

Put light back into sad eyes and make somebody happy.

Bear of the Sun

You came into my time again and enlightened my life.

You held out your hand and asked me to become your wife.

You opened my eyes to the world around me, and you helped me to understand.

How strength and knowledge can dissolve adversity and what it is like to have a real man.

You are a lover, a friend, a partner, and a teacher,

I welcome you back into my world.

Black Steersmen of Kentucky

Stephen Bishop, Matt Bishop and Nick Bransford to name a few.

These are the men of color, guides of the underworld,

Obeyed by alabaster men.

Fearless explorers beneath the earth, removed from class distinction.

Social hierarchy is reversed here in the dark, deep caves of Kentucky.

Black Vest

Why, I asked a stranger, does color matter?

For what sake do you divide?

For pleasure, for pain, for monetary gain?

How do you see me now?

Why, I asked my brother, does color matter?

For what sake do you divide?

For status, for revenge, for repentance of yesterday's sins?

How do you see me now?

Why, I asked my Maker, does color matter?

For what sake do you divide?

For no one, for nothing, from the beginning to the end.

This is how all should see.

Untitled

To rise above the norm

To sing when you feel like crying

To never believe the fabricated

To listen when all others speak

To always ask why

To hold a newborn baby in your arms and listen to this delicate being breathe

To close your eyes and listen to the wind and rain

These things are what make life worthwhile

Body Images

In the mirror of my mind,

I see a different silhouette than society.

I see my body as normal, beautiful and desirable and not at all a deformity.

I am not made to be like everyone else.

I am the product of early genetic engineering.

I am the result of years and years of selection,

Which has brought me to my perfection.

So back off society, and allow me to be me.

The beauty I was meant to be.

Sensations

Chase away the sensations.

I am not ready to care;

Bear your confusion before me and perceive my pain.

Taste the agony on my lips and keep the fear from overflowing.

How can one face himself when pain and despair are there everyday?

Yours is not a new story.

Just learn to pray.

Accepted wisdom is not for everyone.

Circadian Rhythm

Flowing waters, absconding clouds, and gusting winds

The awakening of flowers in the sun or the buzz of hummingbirds wings

The opening of eyes in the morning, the pace of life, and the routines of existence

These are the rhythms we ignore

The beating of a baby's heart

The roar of the ocean tide

The blood that flows and gives us life

These are the rhythms we forget to appreciate

Clifford

In the late hours of September, he was born

The eldest, the strong

Years of fighting for his country

Followed by years of tears, pain, and suffering

Only rest confronts him now

Twenty-six years of needles and pins are no more

The time has come to let him go, to suffer no more

The heart failed, but the soul remained

God came to him in the early light, took his hand, and led him home

Colonized Mind

They look with eyes unsure.

They believe whatever they are told.

They have long-stopped listening to their inner voice.

What is beauty?

Where is right?

Who has a right to an equal life?

Learn to sense with the inner self.

The words men speak are not always untrue.

Their masks conceal the anger inside.

What is one to do?

Corridors of Racism

Walk the narrow corridors of racism

Smell the air of distrust

Taste the sweat of a hardened heart and lose yourself

Ingest the myths of a different race

Fear the possibility of Equality

Contaminate the minds of the younger ones and lose yourself

Walk the narrow corridors of racism

Choke on the misbeliefs that abound

Turn your head to a starving neighbor, and you will lose yourself

Creature of Wings

How wondrous pure flight must be, not like the mechanical flight of man—enclosed in metal, plastic, and fumes—but like the softness of a feather gracefully cutting through the currents.

Navigating the winds, the openness of the sky, and the colors that live there.

The closeness to the Creator of all things.

True masters of flight with gift of song, their keen eyes, and swiftness of motion.

Adorned with colors that could shame a rainbow.

How I long to understand your songs,

See through your eyes, and feel the sky against my skin.

Cry

I lie in the Valley of Shadowed Dreams, and I cry.

I hear the horse's hoofs on God's moistened earth, and I cry.

I felt the earth crumble about me, and I cried.

I gave birth to a baby girl on a frozen morn, and I died.

Dark Images

Dreams and faces of those who endure swim through time.

The mediocre offspring of an unfortunate race are dying at a disturbing rate.

Jobless are the well educated; forgotten are the illiterate.

Augmenting are the homeless; depressed are the working poor.

Babies born with lethargic eyes have no more tears to shed.

God has gone on holiday.

How are we ever to survive?

Dreamworld of My Memory

In the dreamworld of my memory,

There is a land without a single endangered species,

A land where waters run crystal blue and the sun is always in plain view.

It's a place where crowds are not yet known,

Where all animals are free to roam.

Where treasures are buried underground

And where civilized man still abounds.

In the dreamworld of my memory,

There is no old or weak

But acceptability in the mild and the meek.
A place where equality is given to all who live,

Be they male or female, small or big.

Here all things are as I wish until my memory awakens,
and reality is a just a thorn that persists.

Environmental Homicide

Oil spills

Ozone depletion

Endangered species

Auto emissions

Soil erosion

Air pollution

All too common today

How will we be judged by our children's children?

Will they see us as selfish and unconcerned?

Dolphin mutilations

Nuclear waste

Massive garbage dumps and contaminated waterways

Chemical influx

How will we be judged?

Fire of the Fly

Once every year when the summer heat draws near

Power without a cord or plug

Nature's own lightning bugs

Illuminating at the setting of the sun

Fluorescent bodies blinking to nature's tune

Like thousands of tiny musicians in a large dark room

Bringing mystery and magic to all who see

But their magic has calculated days soon all their brilliance will fade

Until this time next year when summer heat draws near

These tiny, beautiful players will again appear

Flames of Remembrance

They gather together as the darkness extends to reminisce of happier days.

The candles are lit and passed on till the light blazes in the night.

Each flame has a name of someone dear.

They are the daughters, the mothers, the sisters, and the grandmothers.

Precious lives were cut short by the hands of those they loved.

For each and every flame, there are shattered dreams, broken hearts,

and tears from those they have left behind.

For those that stay, nothing will ever be the same.

How long must our sisters continue to die before justice cares?

Forever and a Day

Please don't go away; I need you here with me. How can we not be together?

How can we no longer be one?

Remember the days when love knew us,

Remember the nights in each other's arms, and

Remember the times when no one else mattered?

How can you go away?

Please stay forever and a day.

Whatever the problems,

Whatever the pain,

Whatever has come between us, we can put aside again.

I can't believe the love is gone, so I will be here; I will wait for you forever and a day.

Found My Way

He put food on my table

A roof over my head

Clothes on my back

So this is why I say

I'm grateful

I'm thankful

I found my way

He showed me the path of right

He lighted my way

He gave me strength when needed

And that's why I say

I'm grateful

I'm thankful

I found my way

He took the evil and pushed it away

He lifted my heart and soul

So I could be here today

Freedom

Give me mine

Let me experience the wind

Allow me to see through my own eyes

For I desire what others do not want me to find.

Consideration!

Give me mine

Allow me to see the sky and open the gates to independence so that I may be

Self-sufficient, Self-contained, Self-governed, and Self-proclaimed

I must have my freedom to the end.

Future of You

Prepare yourself for the ways of change

Assimilate

Simplify the learning process

Swallow your favoritism and

Realize the potential of others

Scan the possibilities and remember

People speak without tongues

People hear without ears

And what people see is not always the truth

Glass Dancers

Ejected from corpulent clouds, they dance
Transparent images, powerful in presence,
gliding effortlessly across a clear, placid surface
Sliding, they dance
Slipping, they dance
Inevitable slaves of gravity with one purpose
To descend and disappear

Hands and Hearts

How easily one extends a hand to a stranger.

That familiar appendage with universal meaning can strike,

stroke, scold, and grasp—even push away.

Yet how difficult it is to extend one's heart, that shielded life force enclosed in flesh and bone,

the center of secret thoughts, secret emotions, the breast, the bosom, the soul.

In a lifetime, one extends the hand to hundreds but extends the heart to only a few.

Today, I extend not only my hand but a special place in my heart to you.

Gorgonian

The sea fan anchored in the sand

And ocean currents, it withstands

Fleshy skeleton mistaken for a plant

Its tentacles spread out wide to pull its unsuspecting prey inside

Reality Dreaming

Once I heard a scream

A familiar sound injured and far away

Compelled to seek out its source yet terrified of what might be, there in a small corner of time,
I found reality dreaming

Lying in a hardened, disfigured slumber

Like a child waiting for something that never was or will never be

I found reality dreaming

Through tear-filled gaze and semiclosed mind

I extended my hand and felt the despair

Was I the only one who cared?

Hwisprian (Whispers)

Low intonations uttered in darkened rooms
Secrets not for others' ears

Couples entwined in conversation
Hard, weathered throats with sounds unbecoming
Scandals flowing from lip to ear
Minds free from conscience and obligations
Perceiving and still not hearing

I Have You

As long as I have you
I don't need air to breathe
I don't need light to see
I don't need water to quench my thirst
I don't even need to think
All that I need is you

As long as I have you
Your love will see me through
Your arms will lift me up
You fill my every cup.
All that I see is you

As long as I have you
My sky will always be blue
The rain will come and go, and so will the frost and snow
All that I am is because of you

I Mourn the Human Being

I was known to those who once lived as Ashuutee.

I was born in the time of the White Buffalo, and I have traveled the four hills of life. I come to you now to remember, once the land was fresh and full, the plains vast and wild. The mountain view clear and crisp as it kissed the morning sky. The river flowed clean and abundant as it watched the elk and buffalo pass by.

Then, death was still a stranger.

I remember the great chief Black Rock, band chief of the Teton Sioux. I remember Wolf Chief, head chief of the Mandans, and Eagle's Rib, war chief of the Piegan Blackfeet.

I remember the medicine man Isa-Tai, who believed he could make a bulletproof body paint and waged war against the white buffalo hunters.

I remember the mothers like Running Fawn and Eyes that Follow who lost warrior sons in bloodbaths by the thousands.

I remember the children like Little Bird who never knew her father and the elders like Many Moons who never saw home again.

I remember the young maidens like Nishka who never tasted the sweetness of love or the blessed joy of giving birth and the young warriors like Graywolf who never had a chance to hunt the bear, the dear, or the eagle.

I was there. I was there when the Kiowa, Comanche, Cheyenne, and Arapaho were sent to the prison in Saint Augustine, Florida. I mourn the Human Being. His loss was great not only in lives but in language, in craft, in art, and in spirit.

I mourn the Human Being who now sits in a place he does not recognize, who now wears clothes that do not fit. Who now reflects a face unfamiliar to even him. Who now fights a different battle against the fires of water and a sea of despair?

I mourn the Human Being as should you, for his blood also flows through the veins of history.

My face reflects the change. Once beautiful with great power and untamed, now the beauty is gone. Death calls my name. Ashuutee, Ashuutee, Ashuutee.

In My Eyes

You are as close to perfect as they come.

Gentle and compassionate, there are many qualities in you; these are just a few.

You could never do wrong or seem cruel.

The glow of my skin is kept there by you.

You are embedded not only in my memories but also in my heart.

I don't care what others see.

It makes no difference to me.

Your touch weakens me, your eyes mesmerize me, and your voice soothes me.

Only in my fantasies have I felt a love like this.

I realize this is no illusion; with you, there is no more confusion.

Kathy

A quiet beauty, a genuine concern, a strength and individuality that is quite unique

A beauty that she cannot yet see

A fairness found in few

A shyness that will one day fade

Knowledgeable with the ability to teach

A combination that for many is beyond reach

And when time separates us, as time will do

Remember, I will always remember you

Latitude

Respect—Give me mine!

Allow me to experience Life

For I desire what many do not wish me to find

Freedom of Religion

Freedom of Speech

Freedom to Disagree

Options—Give me a choice

Allow me to reveal the sky

No more will my eyes be clouded

Freedom in Education

Freedom to Question

Freedom to be who I was meant to be

Opportunity—I must have mine!

To be self-sufficient

Self-contained

Self-governing

Self-proclaimed

For this one must have Freedom in the Home

Freedom to discipline the young

Freedom to the end

Mississippi Mud Waller

Ex-military who wears a mask of grit and hate.
Underneath it all lies a heart of generosity and deep faith.
A loving man with whom my life is shared.

My soul mate on this unfamiliar road called life.
Never thought I would love like this.
Never dreamed of love returned.

I feel blessed.

Moonlight

The moonlight touches your skin, and it glows like new silver in the dark.

Your passion shows through as transparent as a veil.

You take my hand and pull me close.

Not a word uttered yet my body understands.

Our embrace feels like a summer breeze, refreshing and pleasing.

Under the moonlight, only our love commands.

My Children

Ride, my children!

Ride the fire wings to freedom. Ride!

Clutch your families and start the journey long.

Fear not for you, the eldest of earth's civilized rulers, shall rule again.

Sharpen your senses, listen to the aged, and take advantage of their years.

Heed not the negatives that try to encompass you.

Positivity produces productivity.

Grab life by the nape and hold on.

Ride, my children! Ride!

My Journey

Although my years have grown great and the anger has begun to fade,

Once the rage was massive and consumed my every thought and deed.

Once I wanted to separate myself from everyone and everything.

But now!

Calm has found me.

Understanding speaks to me.

Acceptance has convinced me.

Peace is familiar.

Norman

I sit with you in a place of disguised demise

Where weakened bodies attach to machines to relieve the pain

And lifeless carbon-based units remain

I hold your hand and reminisce of days and holidays we spent together

I search for the strength to let you move on

My selfishness lingers

I want you with me

I want you here

I want you always and forever near

And when that last breath is taken and a shell persists

Know that you will be truly missed

On My Side of the Wall

On my side of the wall

I can hear the songs of the birds, but I can't see their colors

I can hear the children playing, but I can't see their faces

The sun, it shines, but there it does not shine on me

On my side of the wall

Loneliness is my only companion

Beauty and leisure are merely dreams

Happiness is something in a Grimm fairy tale, and humanity has forgotten its purpose

On my side of the wall

Flowers are pictures on a page

The wind blows, but I can't feel a breeze

This world of concrete and stench that I call mine will not induce insanity yet

Peine forte et dure

In the measurements of time,

The innocent are condemned, and the guilty, freed,

A hideous form of execution during earth's premature years.

Unsure of its origin, even more of its end,

This was the way of death for many men

Shattered bones and crushed glands, effervescence of blood from lip to eye.

No mercy was shown to the unfortunate ones.

The carpenter's built devices strong and straight while the villager's stare was carnal and still.

This method of inhumanity did intend to crush out the life of those who sinned.

Peppercorn

Colors may vary, but dark is usually the norm.

Years of mockery endured denying self and kind.

Lies manufacture hidden hates from time to time.

Sleep too long and lose the way.

Smell the stench of confusion and pass it on,

For why should it stop with you this day?

Red Bird

Every evening as the sun loses its light

A Red Bird rests on my porch for the night

Watching my windows as the darkness grows

This Red Bird remains constant, sure, watchful, and pure

And as dawn begins, he flies away

As if he was protecting me until I am again in the light of day

Regretful

We, the so-called civilized creators of a subculture of savagery,
have made the progeny the enemy.

Spawned by a corrupt and confused society, this unaffected child faces with remorse removed
used guns, sex, drugs, and fractured dreams as playthings.

Media spreads the creed of violence like an explosive, involuntary scream.

Invisible fathers and mothers who hate their own flourish.

There is no one place to place the blame.

There is no one face that can wear the shame.

Remember Me

Every time you see a sparrow

Or wish upon a star

Every time a dark corner is brightened by the sun

Remember me

Every time you hear laughter

Anytime your soul feels free

Every time you feel the warmth of a loved one

Remember me

Anytime you feel lucky

Every time you feel at ease

Anytime you feel that you are all alone

Remember me

Reminisce

I begin to reminisce

Of that uncontrollable bliss

Of days and nights I never wanted to end

Me on you

You on me

What ecstasy

So the story goes

When you have had the best

Why bother with the rest?

September

No longer summer and not yet fall, close to winter's blanket chill.

A month of beginnings to endure.

Leaves of amber hues and sun-bright yellows still clinging to limbs of soon-to-slumber trees.

A time of change, month of harvests.

Sapphire's time to shine.

Schools are back in session. No holidays to mention yet. It's a month that deserves respect.

Shanti Knew

Smile of morning

Eyes of warmth

Presence of royalty

Wisdom of young brow

Aurora of sincerity

You will always be a friend to me

Quiet and coy

Gentle in manner and speech

Responsive toward life

Remembering you will bring such glee

You will always be a friend to me

You carry life within

For you have the heart of a dreamer and the hand of an artist

Remember me wherever you may be

You will always be a friend to me

Song of the Sequoias

Named after a great Cherokee leader named Sequoya

You are the splendor of mother earth

The world's largest living monuments stand

Trees of the gods fill the eyes with silent melodies

Their presence echoes their majestic rhetoric

Warming ambers of ageless wonders

Dwarfing the self-proclaimed masters of this earth

Sequoia, you have seen this earth in its infancy

You have seen the sky when it was new

You have felt the anger of the wind and bathed in the torrential rains

Yet you remain

Firm, tall, and strong

You are the living testimonies of time

Spirits

Spirits untamed and misunderstood, teach me

I ask those who have gone before me to guide me

Ancient knowledge reveals your strengths

Remember always

Daughters of forgotten gods

With movements choreographed to a silent tune

Controlled by forces yet unseen, they cling to life

Simple travelers on their way to the next

Stone-Cold Rhythms

Rhythms are all around us—in everything.

This idiom and these regularly occurring motions dictate our hearts,
our minds, and our bodies.

But when these rhythms become unfeeling,
heartless, the damage is done.

Subculture of Savagery

Where the progeny are the enemy

Dehumanizing their prey

Stealing, raping, and murdering, disrespecting all

Unaffected child faces with remorse removed

Guns and drugs and fractured dreams are their playthings

With medias that spread the creed of violence like a plague

With mothers that hate their own

Fatherless children searching, hoping and unsure

Whose responsibility are they now?

Temporal Existence

Nine months after my father's bliss, the knowing of human life, I kissed.

Unprepared for what lay ahead, I suckled. I grew to feel.

We are trained to live for only a short time, eternity never met for me to be.

All around me, time moves. My mortality proven as my life comes in stages.
Love begins. Love ends. I cry. I laugh. I die.

The Vampire Lestat

The gift of darkness comes when the gift of light ends.
Open to me a universe ambiguous in nature and rich in sensations.

The labyrinth of life bores me still; mortal men have taken their toll.
These eyes see with a pessimistic gaze, and my soul is up for grabs.

Lestat, give me those parted lips with moisture removed.
Give to me the teeth, sharp and strong. Embrace me until the deed is done.

Give me the immortal kiss so that I may be reborn.

Time to Go

I didn't think much about it. It never really came to mind.

Until that day when it almost came,
that's when I realized that at any given day, at any given time,
it could be my time to go

Is one ever really ready?

Can one ever be prepared?

When mortality is hardly spoken of

Until that day when it almost comes, that's when you realize that at any given day,
at any given time

It could be your time to go

Perhaps ignorance is best

For one could truly go mad if one knew the very day, the exact time, of their demise

To the Rule

My friends say one day, I will be over you

That it is always darkest before the dawn

But they don't understand

You are the exception to the rule

My family tries to help me with words of advice

They say, "find somebody new."

But they don't understand

You are the exception to the rule

The doctors say it is just a phrase

Depression and medication are the way

But they don't understand

You are the exception to the rule

Lines of Life

I walk between the lines of life

Stumbling along the way

Seeking guidance at each and every turn

With prayer; hope; and a constant, optimistic heart

I walk between the lines of life.

Shades of people, whispers, and screams

Regretting the lost dreams

Cries of joyful pain

I walk between the lines of life again.

Today

I look to see

I listen to hear

I smell to taste

I cry to feel

I live to die

Together

There may come a day when you up and leave.

A time will come when you won't be lying next to me.

Appreciate the time we have together now.

I will be with you as long as God allows.

"Together forever" is not said much these days.

"Here today. Gone today" seems the way.

True Pain

Most of us know nothing of it.

Others understand its way.

We who realize it's only a part of life know that it's here to stay.

Some fear it.

Others cherish it.

Some research it.

Others try to hide from it.

But we would realize there is no true gain without it.

Pain is part of the master plan.

Never really know it and you will never understand.

When Mama Dies

When Mama dies

The winds will no longer blow clean

The sun will cast a constant haze

And the river's flow will blacken and smell

When Mama dies

The clouds will thicken

The air will stiffen

And birds will bear fragile young with wings that cannot soar

When Mama dies

The grass will no longer turn green

The flowers will not bloom

The fields will not flourish

So our babies will perish

When Mama dies

And hope can no longer be seen

The end will have its awakening

White Buffalo

Each season of the new life

The maidens dance and ask the Buffalo to visit

Circles upon circles were drawn; inside were offerings and gifts

The warriors wearing heads and hides chant and ask the Buffalo to visit

Clothe us

Feed us

Shelter us

Those of advanced years sit and pray for the Buffalo to visit

Give us strength

Grant us knowledge

Heal us

Window Rain

Thousands of tiny beads gather on my window, helpless against gravity's strain.

Small ones clench, become larger, and descend.

This is the window rain.

Fallen water from a clouded sky, down and down they descend.

Searching for any surface,

This is the window rain.

Gray days appear.

Sadness awakens in some.

Drops of water alive and untamed,

This is the window rain.

Woman of the Sun

Your plight is known

Your burden seen

Your tear-stained face

Will soon be cleaned

With your head held high

Your energy will soar

Your companion's poverty

Illiteracy and woe

Will be no more

Knowledge and persistence are the shields you must use

To obtain a place in a world

That is still so very confused

Your Heart

Quickly hide your heart for love is near

That thing that others hold so dear

Don't they know hate rides on love's heels?

Ready to pounce; ready to steal

Only a fine line separates the two

A line so delicate it cannot be perceived

But once crossed, it can never be redeemed

So hide your heart if you know what's best

Hide your heart and never put it to the test

Without Me

Don't you dare see a scary movie without me.

Don't you dare sit on the beach and watch the waves without me.

Don't you dare celebrate a birthday or holiday without me or
watch a sunset or play in the rain without me.

I just can't leave you alone. I've tried. I've cried. I've even lied to myself,
and I believe that you shouldn't do anything without me.

When I lose the ability to breathe and my eyes dry up and no longer produce tears,

When statues begin to cry and all birds forget how to soar and when blue leaves the skies,

That is when I know I will no longer need you.

When babies forget how to cry and hope ends,

When rain no longer falls,

That is when I will no longer need you.

Lucille

You gave your all to those you loved

You gave your all to those you knew

You helped so many while you were here and left sweet memories for a few

Sacrifice was your constant companion

You always kept others from harm

Now it is time for you to rest in God's outstretched arms

About the Author

Denise was born in Cincinnati, Ohio. She attended the University of Cincinnati.

Denise was very involved in several Black History Month events at the university, and in 1994, she received the Editor's Choice Award for outstanding poetry from the National Library of Poetry.

Denise is a traveler and has been to Belgium and South Africa.

Printed in the United States
By Bookmasters